Healing Time

Healing Time

by

Marv Ward

Broad River Books
Chapin, SC

Healing Time. Copyright 2020 by Marv Ward. All rights reserved. Printed in the United States of America. No part of this book may be used or reproduced in any manner whatsoever without written permission except in the case of brief quotations embodied in critical articles and reviews. For information please contact Broad River Books, an imprint of Muddy Ford Press, 1009 Muddy Ford Road, Chapin, SC 29036.

Broad River Books

is an imprint of

MuddyFordPress.com

Library of Congress Number: 2020930437

ISBN: 978-1-942081-25-8

Table of Contents

Introduction 3

Thorns 5

First Thursday 7

Carnival of Love 9

The Strawberry Patch 11

Dust 13

Autumn 15

Damaged Goods 17

Into the Unexpected 19

Junk 21

Thanksgiving 23

Healing Time 25

The Swan 27

San Haiku 29

Ode To the Masseuse 31

Michael's Open Mic Night 33

Mourning Music 35

Salve Regina 37

Libretto 39

That Afternoon In the Courtyard 41

I Stood Alone 43

Blue Moonlight 45

REM Rain 47

Calendar 49

Are We There Yet? 51

Reflections After Seeing the Play "Ugly Art" 53

The Fate of Man 55

Totality 57

Pick-Up Lines 59

The Desperate Heart 61

Halo 63

Luncheon 65

I'm Sitting Here 67

The Fencing Match 69

As I Lay Here Tonight 71

Proposal 73

Break Of Day 75

The Wail 77

Hitchhiker 79

Insomnia 81

Seclusion 83

Pied Piper 85

With Apologies to Pele 87

Introduction

Fellow travelers, in this collection, *Healing Time*, poet, musician, troubadour, and minster to all, Marv Ward leads this soul-infected journey in verse and prayer with a heart strummed hard and redemptive words. He reminds us that lives are not shorn of hope even when faces are unrecognizable in reflected waters. With a feverish body of work, he soothes our self-doubt and seasons of despair. In his poem, "Are we there yet?" seekers have questions and what follows must sometimes be, "Where are we now?" Like many of us, the poet wants to know "who the hell is driving the bus?"

In the poem, "Calendar" Ward reveals, "fascination with times unceasing/and unyielding passing is the only truth we hold." In "Carnival of Love" we ride the tilt-a-whirl of longing." We hear "the ocean's roar" in "Blue Moonlight" and watch the tidal shift in the line "the morning after the night before." In these poems, yes, there is delirium but there are also fertile reminders of the openness we must hold onto. In his poem, "Autumn," he implores us to "listen to the whippoorwill's call for seeds to be planted."

Marv Ward is a believer of dreams, of passion and of love, of Morpheus, of the mysteries of time, but also of bedevilment and encumbrances. He scribbles truth like a diarist in "As I lay Here Tonight" and admits, "I search for a space/where our hearts/could meet as one, hold each other/and dance across the eternal abyss/to the music of the spheres." In the poem, "Hitchhiker" he balances the past and future with the line, "the baggage I carry contains my choices," but confesses, "I long to be unfettered." And in the title poem, "Healing Time," he whispers to damaged souls that the time for healing has begun. With that, his poem, "Into the Unexpected" escorts us through the dark corridor," while the short piercing "Libretto" leaves us "gaping in wonder/never knowing the truth."

His poems are piping with sound; wails, a steam-released collection where the calliope cautions "the desperate heart/knows no fear/but is afraid to be alone." Marv Ward's poems wound and heal with a lyrical voice, and the triumphant refrain is that regardless of pain, loss, dust, and longing, somehow, we remain who we are supposed to be. All we have is our ability to give thanks when "night looms" and to move forward in our "endeavor to persevere." This collection is a full moonrise for a thirsty soul.

Tim Conroy

Author, *Theologies of Terrain*

Thorns

If you love the rose,
be prepared to be stuck by
a thorn now and then.

First Thursday

Echoes of delirium reverberate through the silence.
The depth of platitudes widens
      and reality disappears
           into the abyss of geniality.
In desperation,
      I touch her cheek,
           but the warm soft embrace of her
      countenance
      belies the distance to her heart
and I reluctantly withdraw
      to the shell of acceptance
           that hides my despair.
The cold night air piques my senses
      and I wander,
           aimlessly,
                searching for direction,
                      but my destination is lost.
      I stop and stare into the heavens
           as
echoes of delirium reverberate through the silence,
           and walk on.

Carnival of Love

Dislocated between reality and perception,
    confused,
        about in which realm I lie.
The notes of the pleasure of existence calliope
    plays a contrapuntal melody
        against the pain of being.
I try to gather my wayward thoughts
    as they stray among the carnival sideshow of emotions
        that define my love.
I ride the tilt-a-whirl of longing
    destined
        to push reset for another trip around
            as I ponder the odds of winning the ring toss.
Too late, I realize the odds are stacked
    against me
        another circuit has begun
            and my destiny is ordained.
The hand is dealt
    and I wonder if I should cash in
    or stand pat till the river
I call
    and wait.

The Strawberry Patch

We suddenly heard the old man's voice
    piercing the summer Sunday silence.
I jumped up and followed my father
    out the back door
        to see my grandfather,
            his old double barrel shotgun in hand,
    chasing two Brahma bulls out of the strawberry patch.
Yelling and waving the weapon,
    grandfather cursed the beasts
    and chased after them through the dusty afternoon heat.
"We better help him before he hurts himself," my father said,
    and we ran to the old man's side.
The bulls having eaten their fill
    lazily retreated to pasture.
"Fafa" surrendered his pursuit and went back inside
    to his chair.
But now as I
    stand alone in the field
        holding my rifle,
    trying to steady my stance,
        not being able see the target through the scope,
            knowing I dare not pull the trigger,
I realize I am that old man
    trying to protect my garden
        from the invasion of time and predatory malice,
    still believing in my imagined capabilities,
        unwilling to give up my perceptions and dreams
        and face the new reality of age.
The doc says it's cataracts and I'll have to have surgery
    to restore my vision
    but I doubt my visions will ever be what they have been.

I gaze into my future
    and wonder what it will behold.
It is so hard to give up on the years of aspirations,
    unfulfilled longings
        incomplete opuses
            and unresolved desires
                and stare reality in the face
    a face I hardly recognize in the mirror anymore.
In this ebb tide of life
    I try to hold my own against the current
        and search for islands of being to cling to
            to stave off the inevitable
    and hope that someone will run to my side
before I
    hurt myself
        and help me
            rescue my strawberry patch.

Dust

The stark light on my lawn
    revealed
        the bare spots and dust.
My feet were enveloped in the cloud as I walked
    I cried here I am
        but my soul was lost
            and the dust kept rising.

Autumn

My leaves are starting to turn,
    my bark has gotten crusty and rough,
    the sap doesn't flow as swiftly
        as it once did.
The change in the air signals the coming transformation.
    I have come to the autumn of my existence.

As the seasons of my life evolve,
    I look back,
        ponder the spring.
Crisp,
    fresh and new
        filled with buds of lust that flowered into love.
Love,
    that was nourished by the violent storms
        of passion.
As ecstasy's lightning flashed
    amid the thunder of misplaced heartbeats,
        experience blossomed into knowledge
        and grew into awareness.

Then came the long sultry summer of living,
    wafting
        from the lush green fields of complacent pleasure,
    to the barren deserts of disdain
        parched memories of loss
        the drought of desire.
I perpetually walked across the dry, cracked landscape of rejection
    searching
        for every oasis of acceptance and caring
        to quench my thirst for affection.
I lingered at some wells, until I was slacked,
    but never tasted the true sweet water of love.

And now as I face the inevitable advance
        of the cold dark winter's sleep
                I long for one more spring
A brief renewal
A respite
           To lay once more
                    in fields of passion's flowers
                          and feel the warm touch of ardor.
Listen to the whippoorwill's call for seeds to be planted
                and have one last tango in the moonlight,
                        before the sun sets forever.

Damaged Goods

My life suddenly feels like a forlorn love letter
        undelivered
                marked return to sender,
A package, frayed at the edges,
        storm tossed and rain soaked,
                whose seal has been broken,
        refused at the door
                stamped damaged goods.
Prospects for the future are disappearing
        even as each blessed sunrise
                is experienced and rejoiced.
The thought of eternal night looms
I recite with fervor the words of Dylan Thomas
        and have and will
                rail with all the strength I have,
as I fight to hold off the unseen
        forces and weariness that try to possess me.
I re-tape the package,
        readdress a new envelope
                and wait for divine delivery
                        to a new destination.

Into the Unexpected

Awake before dawn
I stumble into the day
      through a dark corridor
           of my being.
Searching for the light,
      I induce my body to rise
        with caffeinated potions
and dull the pain of temporal existence
      with baked grains and sugar.
I stand and face
      the sunrise
as an explorer on the shore of a vast sea
      wondering what lies beyond,
           but unsure if I want to get my feet wet.
Then with a last bite of resolve,
      I plunge ahead
           into the unexpected.

Junk

Standing in my kitchen
        clutching my junk
                and staring out my window at the new day,
I am perplexed at the appalling amount of trappings
that have become slung around my neck like an albatross,
        yet I still deem too precious
                to cast into oblivion
                        and rid myself of
        these tempestuous burdens.
Each belonging
        possessed by a memory deeply ingrained
                or dream
                        yet unfulfilled
                              clings to my being
        and leeches to the very soul of my bones.
My ego cherishes these playthings,
I believe that I can control the desires
        to paint my existence,
                illuminate hidden meanings
                        and mold them into new creations.
But all I end up doing is standing naked in the sun
        squeezing the jewels of inspiration
                and bleeding.
I have to wash my hands.

Thanksgiving

The distance between what was
      and what is
           is so close,
                and yet so far.
Dreams do not evaporate
      with a change of atmosphere,
           but the realization of them dims
      in the stark light of reality,
           when the conversations of plans
                are replaced with prayers of hope.
Many times, I threw the coins of the I Ching
      and was told to persevere,
           but now
                that fortune is all too real,
                    the only option is perseverance.
But I will embrace the prediction
      and revel in new chances to feel,
           sunlight on my face,
               the caress of a lover,
                   fresh air in my lungs.
and I will strive to envelop my soul
      in the art of living well
           and endeavor to, once again, persevere.

Healing Time

He raised his arms to the Heavens
    and began to sing
        as the casket was lowered.
His voice tore through the sobbing stillness,
    an angel's trumpet
        calling her home.
I grasped his hand
    and steadied his reeling presence.
No eyes fell on him,
all were transfixed by the moment.
As his last note echoed
    through the trees,
        carried aloft
            on celestial winds.
We rose in silence
    and faced the future.
All farewells had been whispered
and the time for healing
    had begun.

The Swan

You sit in your cell
      staring at the walls that life has enveloped you in,
          trying to write your haiku.
When suddenly fluttering through an open window
      the most beautiful swan in the lake
         embraces you with her wings,
         holds you within her eternal love,
     wipes away your tears,
     kisses your soul
         and gives you hope for a new tomorrow.
You bow to her countenance,
     wallow in her warmth
         and shudder at the possibilities,
but know that flight of love can never be
     and pick up the pen.

San Haiku

On the summit peak
holy men in high places
walk through a meadow

Across the cold sky
behind the dismal gray clouds
the sun is shining

Beauty to the eye
beware the painted damsel
deadly to the heart

Ode To the Masseuse

Petite and lithe
    yet strong and deft
        she has a magician's slight of hand.
Her hands are the keys to heaven.
My flesh shudders
    as her touch reaches deep
        into the stiffness that engulfs my body
            and eases the pain of existence.
With surgical precision,
    she finds the troubled tendons
        and forces them to relinquish their hold on my suffering.
She strums my body like a taut strung guitar,
My muscles sing choruses of relief
    and moan in ecstasy.
But within the pleasure
    lives a dragon.
Her touch is addictive as the poppy's flower.
The more she gives the more you want
    and the desire leads to madness.
Trips to the pawn shop,
    borrowing from the mortgage money
        anything
            to feel her healing hands once more.
And yet,
    as she kneads your pain,
you dream of dancing with her
    across a moonlight sky
        into an ocean of bliss,
until she taps your forehead
    and says "hour's over."

Michael's Open Mic Night

After the hurricane,
      a new moon pierced the evening sky,
night birds warbled
      across the ebbing tide,
the fearful gales calmed
      to enticing breezes of normality
          and our hearts opened
      and sang,
          to fulfill our desires.
After the hurricane,
      love blossomed from the spores
          of destruction
      spread by the tornadic tempest
      across the resolve of our souls
          and we embraced our newfound passions.
After the hurricane,
      we drank
          and toasted our fortunes
      two-stepped and shuffled through the darkness
            till the light of a new dawn
                illuminated our lives
      and we could
begin again.

Mourning Music

Tears fall from the sky and I hear the King's moan,
But rain can't wash away the pain that we've known
Gray Monday morning the big Papa wrote,
Yet, we all took solace when Mama hit the note.
Another Manic day as Blue as it can be
Even Parrot Heads in an LA haze are lost at sea.
Yes, it's Stormy and it always gets me down,
But I can chase away the sadness with all this Monday sound.

Salve Regina

She was a Natural Woman
        fettered by a Chain of Fools
                who demanded Respect
                      and implored us to Think
                      about our actions.
She was a Do Right Woman
        who wasn't afraid to say Baby I Love You
                and tell you she Never Loved a Man the way she loved you.
The Queen is gone but she still reigns supreme,
Cruise on down that Freeway of Love in your Pink Cadillac your Highness
        and know you will be forever loved and cherished.

Libretto

I need a libretto for life's
      opera.
The melodies' meanings get blurred
      by the passions
           of the performances
and I am left gaping in wonder
      never knowing the truth.

That Afternoon In the Courtyard

The pool was full of grass now
    but we waded in anyway
        bathing under a bluebird spring sky
            and floated on the words of poetic prophets
                who sang songs of futures past.
I watched a pair of doves cooing under the myrtle branches,
    dancing love's tango in the dappled sunlight.
I listened to the siren sagas being sung and
    echoed back
        my own refrain
            lost deep in dreams of hidden meanings,
    but was startled back to reality
        by the screams of sudden silence.
I opened my eyes
    only to find that the doves and you had flown
        and wondered if I had hit a wrong note
            or if I should have sung,
but life without dreams and song
    is no life at all.

I Stood Alone

I stood alone
  in a crowd.
Suddenly,
    she grasped my hand
      and clutched it tight.
She whispered in my ear and kissed my cheek.
    I wanted to pull her to me
      and hold her in my arms forever
        but knew I could not.
She then withdrew once again
   into the crowd
     I reluctantly let loose her hand
  and once again
I stood alone

Blue Moonlight

Red wine, orchids and blue moonlight,
the music, the incense, a sultry summer night.
You caught my eye with a knowing glance,
I asked if you'd like to take a chance.
We shared an evening of pure delight
with red wine, orchids and blue moonlight.

The morning after the night before,
I wanted to hold you even more.
My dreams were filled with those gypsy eyes,
your raven hair, your sorceress disguise.
You held my hand by the ocean's roar,
the morning after the night before.

Then evening came, and away you pranced,
another's song had made your heart dance.
You left my side, let loose my hand,
never looked back as you ran to join the merry band.
Fate rolled the dice and I lost my chance,
to sail love's ship on the seas of our romance.

And now the tide has ebbed and washed away
all but the memories of that day.
I stand alone on the shore and stare at the sea
remembering that time that you loved me,

and steel my journey, through this endless night,
with red wine, orchids and blue moonlight.

REM Rain

Lightning flashes through the soft summer rain,
through distant thunder I hear your voice again.
I feel you lying close to me
I wake and call your name
but there is no answer
to love's haunting game.
These feelings are just illusions,
brought on by the confusions
of magic from the past.
But in fleeting morning moments
I dream forever they would last.
As the storm of love dies
and the tide of life turns
in the time before waking
the fire of our romance still burns.
I could awaken and quell my hearts beat
but I cling to the shadows, hide under the covers
and revel in the heat.

Calendar

How futile and flawed
    the fallacy of time as we know it.
With pompous sanctimony
    we mark and measure it,
        thinking the universe will align
            with our egotistical perception
                of the evolutions of existence.
In reality
    light and dark are all we know,
        with subtle nuances on the edges,
            married to our instincts to survive
                life's mystery and magic.
Conjecture is our only awareness of time;
    speculation of what has past,
        dreams of events yet to be revealed.
Fascination with time's unceasing
    and unyielding passing
        is the only truth we hold
    and yet
        we constantly pray for it to stop.
Why do we attempt to gauge universal cycles?
Perhaps to satisfy a deep hidden need
    for some ethereal sense of security,
        sanity, or superiority?
Psychedelic gurus tell us to,
    "Be Here Now"
but none of us is positive
    what "Now" really is.
The future does not exist without the past
    so, who can be certain where "Now" lies.

You can not find it on a calendar, or clock, or sundial, for as Mr. Miller said
"time keeps on slipping, slipping, slipping, into the future."

Are We There Yet?

Are we there yet?
Where are we now?
I suddenly feel like I have been awakened
       from a long sleep
              in the back of a car
                      traveling a monotonous interstate
       for 50 years
              with only the faint memory of a radio
                      playing in my dreams.
I look around and do not recognize the landscape
       or my fellow travelers
              and who the hell is that driving?
Why haven't we reached our destination?
Are we there yet?
Where are we now?
Has our moral compass been shattered,
or is it malfunctioning from alien interference?
What happened to the quest,
the journey,
       the drive
              to change
                      our destiny
where are the blithe spirits
       that danced naked in golden gate
              and slithered through the mud at Woodstock
                      with dreams of new tomorrows,
who burned their identities and brassieres on statehouse
steps?
Are we there yet?
Where are we now?

Did we get lost
        when parenthood and daily routine
                invaded our lives?
Was it a wrong turn
        or have we been overcome
                with the fear of only having
                      a one-way ticket?
Are we there yet?
Where are we now?
Why hasn't that seed
        planted by the rebellious youth of new awareness
                blossomed into the utopian jungle of Rousseau.
Was it shorn by unrelenting doubt,
        or by the fascist gardeners of complacency?
Are we there yet?
Where are we now?
And who the hell is that driving the bus!

Reflections After Seeing The Play "Ugly Art"

As I sit by the pool staring at my reflection,
    it is not love that I feel.
            Narcissus, I am not.
Nor do I feel loathing, disgust or doubt
    although I am sometime my own Nemesis.
But instead I am overcome with wonder.
Is this a true image of who I am?
    A portrait of reality
        or like Pollack's droplets
            a matter of perception,
                interpretation.
I think of Gray's painting,
    kept covered in an attic
        so that his inner truth would not be revealed,
but the poet is a burlesque performer
    dancing behind feathered fans of entendre,
        tempting readers to look closer
            to see what is hidden,
                but in the end, stands and bares all to the throng.
If I touch the liquid
    the image distorts but it is still recognizable.
The ripples in one's life do not change who we are
    but they may change how some perceive the image
        and the reaction to it.
Personality is the element that changes
    the play of light and shadow that is our portrait.
        It can attract and repel,
            mesh or clash
                create a cult or a pariah.
                  But without it, no one would come to the gallery,
    monochromatic life has a very small following.

I see that my reflection has changed drastically
    from the impressions in my memories.
The waters of life's river flow,
    sometimes swiftly over turbulent rapids
      or with a slow crawl along a delta plain
        but can never be recaptured once they have gone under the bridge.
Memories are resilient, and ever present
    but cannot create a dam to stop the passing tide.
Nonetheless,
as I sit in my daze of wonderment,
it is my reflection
and regardless of its ripples, perceptions and persona
it is who I am.

The Fate of Man

I need to find closure
        from this indecent exposure
                to my mind
                from thoughts, so unkind.
        From inane protesters,
        animal molesters
               and demons who malign my dreams.
I need some relief from the pain of living
        amongst the ungiving,
                beliers of beliefs
                soul thiefs
        who feed on the tormented screams.

I must escape from this prison of fear
        of words that I hear
                spewing from the lips of lunacy
                choruses of redundancy
        maleficent madness
        locked in sadness
                by the chains of the foul and uncouth.
I have to break the shackles of moral pretenders
        sexual offenders
                political ghouls
                leading legions of fools
        seeking to bury the truth.

How can I clog the spigot,
>of the flowing bigot
>>and the polluted stream
>>of maniacal schemes?
>Rhetorical bile,
>platitudes in a pile
>>that threaten to dissolve our being.
Flush it away
>don't let the poison stay
>>to fester and rot
>>all the good that has been wrought
>all the beauty there is worth seeing.

I shall rise up and stand
>fiercely demand
>>that peace shall abide,
>>quelling the tide,
>of a culture of hate
>they wish to create,
>>to entomb the spirit of life.
I will laugh in their face,
>hold fast to the place,
>>where love is real,
>>kindness can heal,
>and people are free from eternal strife.

Totality

The conflict that challenges my serenity is cleaving my psyche.
I am plagued by images in my dreams
that morph between angels and demons,
I sleep in fear and ecstasy
torn between terror and desire.
The songs of the trees are growing fainter
and the elves have not called me to dance since the last
solstice moon.
I am beginning to dread the winter's stillness,
that long cold nights sleep
that I know is coming.
I turn to my unfilled longings and memories of shattered
dreams
to stoke the fire of my soul,
but there is no heat left in those ashes,
and I am afraid that I will never kindle a new flame.
I contemplate the meanings and mysteries
and realize that there is no knowledge to offer an explanation.
Beliefs are but a refuge
to assuage the fear of the unknown.
when in essence we are surrounded by all truth and knowledge,
but are blind to the universal wisdom.
The light of the soul always shines but may be eclipsed by
life's shadow.
But alas all this, does little to quell the turmoil of existence
and the thoughts of its demise
without realizing the one essential of being,
true love.

Pick-Up Lines

If I abandoned the blood-stained shroud
that cloaks my true identity,
    would you look behind the curtain?
If I lay down the hammer
I use to pound the unrelenting confusion,
    will you speak?
If I whisper the secret meaning
of the code that will unlock my destiny,
    will you open the door?
If I touch the edge of your razor wit
and bleed on your understanding,
    will you forgive me?

The Desperate Heart

The desperate heart
    aches and bleeds and yearns.
The desperate heart
        never learns.
The desperate heart
    faces the storm of unrelenting misery
        and cries hope.
The desperate heart
    wanders in the carnival at night
        but doesn't see the lights
            doesn't hear the music.
The desperate heart
    stares at its reflection in the blade of the knife.
The desperate heart
    screams in its sleep
        and wakes to a cold reality.
The desperate heart
    tries to quench its fire with alcohol
        and fans the flames with desire.
The desperate heart
    knows no fear
        but is afraid to be alone.

Halo

As we sat dining
    al fresco
        in the glade by the pond,
the evening sun of the Maxfield Parrish sky
    streamed through your hair
        illuminating your halo
            that fairies dance on above your head.
Their songs entranced my mind
        captivating my soul
    and I saw your lips part
        and my heart was surrendered.
And in that glowing ray of light
    shining through the night
        I saw
            your face.
And then I knew,
    at last,
        the time has come to pass,
    and I have found
        the place I could stay forever.

Luncheon

All alone in the café
watching lovers eat,
I slowly digest the day.

I'm Sitting Here

I'm sitting here waiting
counting every tick of the clock
living in lost limbo
until life's secret doors unlock
trapped in a purgatory of desire
without a match
no flame to light the fire

I'm sitting here watching
the retrospective of my time,
reliving the encounters,
some profane some sublime
I cry through scenes that I regret
pause and chuckle
at jokes that haven't happened yet

I'm sitting here listening
for songs I cannot hear
singing words and music
of truth as they appear
hoping I still have a chance
to find a partner
and be able to share one last dance

I'm sitting here dreaming
of what may lie beyond
starring at the reflections
and ripples across the universal pond
I wonder if the water's warm or cold
and if in I dive
will the end or beginning I behold.

The Fencing Match

I know the game is so much more than
parry and lunge,
    parry and lunge.
        parry and lunge.
The foils must meet
   and slide,
       glide along each other's path
      chime with the union
        again and again
          until withdrawn
            to en garde.
But each position is most important
     and must maintain its integrity,
        so there is no compromise.
The feet must correspond
     and dance
        the ballet of engagement
          drawing the partners close,
            then aback,
              near then far,
     until proper placement is conjoined
and the match is consummated
     with a final joyful
        thrust.
            The ultimate touche,
   when,
      with a sigh,
masks are removed,
    hands clasp,
       eyes meet
          and the game is complete.

As I Lay Here Tonight

As I lay here tonight
chasing the thoughts of your countenance
that are racing through my being
I search for a space
where our hearts
could meet as one,
hold each other
and dance across the eternal abyss
to the music of the spheres.
a soft zephyr caressing our souls
as we are carried,
drifting,
on a new tide of experience,
splashing and laughing
in a moonlit sea of endearment.
but suddenly
with no warning
you disappear
leaving only ripples and reflections for me to follow
through my dreams.
As I lay here tonight,
waiting for the embrace of Morpheus
pervaded by his lyrical songs of slumber,
I see you rising from the depths
holding my cheek in your hand
and pressing your lips to mine.
Your hot breath
melts my inner being
as I flow into a puddle of
malleable clay
waiting to be shaped by your desires.
desires unknown and hidden
from my eyes.

As I lay here tonight
soaring aloft
on the winds of passion
I quickly fall back to earth
grounded, burdened and
overcome with the encumbrance
of self-doubt that exists
in my tattered libido,
flying with Icarus's wings
I battle to keep it unseen,
unnerved by a time
when I will have to stand uncloaked
next to your glowing aura
and all would be revealed.
How will I be perceived in your eyes
I wonder what vision
your heart is searching for
and if I can become your partner.
As I lay here tonight
awaiting the inevitable
darkness to close my eyes.
bedeviled and bewitched
by the prospect of an unrequited life,
I still dare to aspire
to be the hand that wipes away your tears
and the heart that holds your love.
Am I trapped in madness or delusion
I know not,
but I can't help but to dream
as I lay here tonight.

Proposal

To gaze upon your face,
hold you in warm embrace,
so that I may see and feel your soul
to feel your breath upon my skin,
have you close to me again,
is my life's one and only goal.

I feel empty when we part
with a lonely hollow heart
I count the minutes until once more
I again can hold your hand
and together we shall stand
on the threshold of ecstasy's door.

Come my dear and walk with me
through all of eternity
let us take the journey together for all time
find the realm where we can be
manifest our destiny
and share the joy of love sublime.

Break Of Day

Glorious glare of the morning sun,
beautiful blare of a new day begun,
fills my eyes and ears with the symphony of life
enraptures my senses and eases the strife.
Cool zephyr caresses my brow,
the wind of change blows through me now
I pause and stand, smile and chuckle within
to know my time has not come to an end.
I breath deep to inhale the joy
That my mind and limbs I can still employ.
I can still tempt fate and take a chance
beg love for just one more dance
and if I trip and fall, flat on my face
at least my soul will be in the race.

The Wail

A foundling
    left in a basket
        at death's door,
  abandoned by fate,
      searching for solace
          in dire circumstance.
Crying for a helping hand,
    a warm touch to allay the fears,
      a cozy comforter
        to embrace and cling to.
The winds of destiny
    blow cold through the long dark night
and the body craves
    the heat of a kindred soul.
From the basket,
    a desperate scream
        to be uplifted one final time.
        held in the arms of passion
          and feel the fire of ardor,
before the tolling bell is answered
    the door is opened
        the basket removed
          and the chance for love is lost.

Hitchhiker

The baggage that I carry contains my choices,

the chains I wear that have been forged by my deeds,

weigh heavy on me now in the closing stretch of the race.

I long to be unfettered,

so that I may glide with grace to the finish line

but alas,

I lumber and drudge

unable to free my soul of its burdens.

I pause often now to catch my breath

and look down the road ahead.

The distant destination is shrouded in fog

and once again it is starting to rain on the parade.

The path is becoming muddy but there is no turning back

and I must slog through to the end.

I stick out my thumb

and hope to be picked up,

ride out the journey with less hardship,

but as a driver slows and pulls close,

I am told I have too much junk for the trunk

as they turn and speed away.

Insomnia

I often seek the solitude of silence,
when the only sound I hear is the music playing in my head.
But true silence cannot be found,
the universe is perpetually turning like an old wax disc
and nature constantly plays a symphony for our soul.
Go and sit in the depths of a snow-covered forest
and listen.
Even within the sanctity of that snow and pine cathedral,
you will hear the earth spinning.
So, sleep, sleep deep in the arms of Morpheus,
let his Lyrical songs assuage your fears.
Lie still in the warm embrace,
until the next awakening and the return of
perpetual tears.

Seclusion

Solitarily seeking solace,
    I slide into the sublime sense of sanctity
        that seclusion supplies.
I supplant my solvency
    with secreted sensations of sexuality
that stumble into the sudden secession of satisfaction,
        only to see my sanity
            slipping away.

Pied Piper

Celestial piper play me a note

upon which my soul can float

across the breadth of time and space

to the sanctuary of love's embrace.

Send me sailing on an arpeggio sea

adrift to an island where my spirit can be free,

unfettered by earthly chains,

released from the burden of life's mortal pains.

Caress my heart with a gentle tone

so, I will not fear the time alone.

Sooth my anxiety with a flutter of breath

calm my nerves as I approach death.

Celestial piper play me a tune

but make it a long one that doesn't end too soon.

With Apologies To Pele

The flaming magma of my soul
      feels the tears
           of my unrequited passion and
      erupts
spewing pieces of my existence
      across my universe.
Lust lava flows
      from fissures in my heart
           searing the landscape of my life,
      then hardens
           to jaded stone
                  sealing the essence of my being within
forming another
      deserted island
           in the desolate sea of love.